THIS IS THE DAY

100 REFLECTIONS ON LIVING AND GIVING

JAMES R. HALLAM

DEDICATED TO ALL THOSE WHO DESIRE TO
MAKE THE WORLD A BETTER PLACE.

INTRODUCTION

You have amazing gifts. You possess the power to bring light, hope and compassion to yourself and your human family, to make the world a more loving, caring, peaceful place. We all do. Too often, however, our gifts go unacknowledged and unused.

Life can be busy and difficult. We have conflicting priorities. We are overwhelmed by our personal problems and the problems of the world. We don't have time or energy to think about our gifts let alone cultivate them. We shove them to the back of the closet and forget they are there.

In my own life, I often find that when I am feeling distracted, distressed, exhausted, or hopeless, reflecting on the gifts I have and how I want to use them revives my spirit. In the pages of this book, I will share some of the words, stories, and ideas that, over the years, have helped me refocus on what is important and adjust my attitude.

I hope that these offerings, along with my personal ruminations, will encourage you to engage in introspection, challenge you to make choices in line with your values, and inspire you to realize the fullness of your humanity. Ultimately, I hope this book will serve as a resource for meditating on your own gifts and provide the motivation you need to make the most of them.

This book is designed to meet you where you are. It is not a book to read through in one sitting. The entries are deliberately short, and self-contained; they will be most useful if you aim to read just one or two a week, allowing the questions to simmer in your mind. Likewise, there is no need to read the entries in order. Feel free to flip through the pages to find one that resonates with you on that particular day, at that particular time. Perhaps you will find that one entry becomes a touchstone that you return to again and again.

It is my firm belief that life is dynamic, that change is always an option, and that it is never too late to realize our potential. As you spend time with this book and think more deeply and intentionally about your gifts, you will begin to see opportunities to practice them in your life. Seize these opportunities to turn insight into action! The most profound and complete fulfillment, in my experience, comes from living and giving our gifts on a daily basis.

1

*This is the day that the Lord has
made. Let us rejoice and be glad in it.*

Psalm 118:24

We have the power to decide what we will do with
the sacred gift of this day. Will we approach it with a
positive attitude, or will we dwell in darkness and
negativity? Will we live this day with understanding,
acceptance, and compassion or will we become
entangled in prejudice, judgment, and self-
centeredness?

How will you live this gift? How will you celebrate
this day? The choice is yours!

2

*"How wonderful it is that nobody
need wait a single moment before
starting to improve the world."*

Anne Frank

We often think we have no power to change the world. But all of us do. It does not have to involve a huge or extraordinary effort. It does not require a production. Every loving, caring act, no matter how small or seemingly ordinary, makes a difference. Every smile, hug, affirmation, and kindness can touch a life. It becomes part of a wave of positive energy that has no end.

What are you waiting for?

3

In 1969, David O. Woodyard's book, *To Be Human Now*, was published. Over the years, I have returned to this book many times. Much of what Woodyard shares was meaningful to me when I read his book in graduate school and much remains relevant today.

For Woodward, religion is actualized through action and experience. "Prayer," he writes, "is not so much what we say to God but what we do on behalf of our neighbor."

"Unconditional engagement with my neighbor in the manner of Christ," he suggests, "is an act of worship."

"Wherever you find yourself and another person is a temple," he notes, "it's the most real holy ground you will ever know."

How do you live your religion on a day-to-day basis?

4

*Watch out and guard yourselves
from every kind of greed, because
your true life is not made up of the
things you own, no matter how rich
you may be.*

Luke 12:15

I once saw a TV ad that promised if you bought a certain product, you would save money and be able to buy more stuff! Our culture often glorifies the accumulation of material goods. The more we have, the more successful we are. But is building a meaningful life grounded in what we accumulate?

"For your heart," Jesus taught, "will always be where your riches are." (Luke 12:34) Meaning comes from how we share the riches of the heart, how we show our love and caring to those in need.

Are you, as Jesus urges us to be, concerned about our human family? Do you seek to alleviate the suffering caused by hunger, homelessness, sickness, and imprisonment?

5

I had the opportunity to attend an Ocean City Pops concert while on summer vacation. It was an excellent show; the talent of the performing artists was on full display. What gifts they had and what a gift for them to share their music with others.

I found myself pondering my own gifts. What do I give to the world? Am I making it a better place through the giving of my gifts?

What about you? Do you sing, write, dance or play a musical instrument? Are you kind and generous on a daily basis? Do you have relationships where you share your love? Do you support causes either financially or through the investment of your time? What gifts are you giving to the world?

6

"The first duty of love is to listen."

Paul Tillich

Have you ever wanted someone to listen to you, but sensed that they were only pretending to be interested? That they were too busy or indifferent to truly hear you? How did you feel? Discounted? Devalued? Disappointed? Remember this feeling and the next time another person wants to give you the gift of their story, give them the gift of your presence in return.

7

Nikki Mirghafori writes about the Buddha's teachings concerning words and speech. "Right speech," she reminds us, "is abstaining from lying, divisive speech, abusive speech, and idle chatter." It is "timely, true, gentle, beneficial, and spoken with a mind of good-will."

Our words can be a tremendous gift to a person, or they can be destructive, causing hurt and pain.
Have you ever pondered the power of the words you speak?

Pay attention to what you say, when you say it, and with what intention. How would it impact your communications and relationships if you worked to cultivate "right speech"?

8

"Be a little kinder than is necessary."

R. J. Palacio, Wonder

Kindness can be an affirming, transforming gift, but it is not complicated. In an article, Sukhman Rekhi and Tchiki Davis, define kindness as "a genuine and sincere way of giving your time and intention to someone else through compassion, time, generosity, and care for the benefit of helping others."

How kind are you? Consider, what would it look like to be "kinder than necessary"? Why wouldn't you be?

9

Lying on his deathbed, Baron von Hugel called his favorite niece to his side and whispered in her ear these words that had guided his life:

"Caring is everything. Nothing matters but caring."

I have tried to be guided by these words in my own experiences as well. As a campus minister at the University of Pennsylvania, I had von Hugel's quote printed at the top of my stationary as a reminder to self and an invitation to others.

What a difference we can make on planet Earth by genuinely caring, by giving the gifts of empathy, acceptance, understanding, and love to all.

10

My wife and I were walking on the Ocean City boardwalk when we decided to browse in the Ocean Treasures store. I was looking at various plaques when one caught my eye. It simply said: "Be still."

In the midst of a hectic schedule, those words spoke to me. They were a gift, a reminder about self-care and the need to pause, see, hear, and wonder. That same day I sat on the beach watching the waves break on the shore and listening to the agitated surf. I was just being and not doing. This meditative escape from a demanding world was a marvelous gift.

Do you accept the gift of stillness?

11

Watching a video of author and former pastor, Rob Bell, I was struck by three small words: "You are rich." All of us are, of course, rich in human gifts. But so many of us living in America today are also rich in material wealth.

On a mission trip to Haiti, I met a number of displaced Haitians. We were there to construct 8' x 12' sheds for them. The spaces were small and minimal, but the people I spoke with expressed gratitude and proudly called them home.

Too often we take our abundance for granted. We focus on ourselves and what we don't have or what we'd like to have more of. What if we were to refocus on giving thanks for what we do have and sharing those resources, even if limited, with others? How would this make a difference in the world? In our own lives?

How are you sharing your riches?

12

*"Someday, after we have mastered the
winds, the waves, the tides and gravity,
we shall harness the energies of love.
Then for the second time in the history
of the world, man will have discovered
fire."*

Teilhard de Chardin

I am an avid consumer of the news. I like to be
informed about what is happening in the world. But I
have to admit that the ugliness and toxicity I
encounter often feels overwhelming. It is shocking to
see the depth of inhumanity, brutality, and hatred we
perpetrate on one another. Will we, I wonder, ever
learn the art of living in peace?

I know that we have it within us. We are people of
light with the capacity for love. Teilhard de Chardin
challenges us to harness that love and use it to change
the world.

Let the fire of love burn away your anger, hatred, and
resentment.

13

*"When you arise in the morning,
think of what a precious privilege it
is to be alive—to breath, to think, to
enjoy, to love."*

Marcus Aurelius

Think of it! Life is a *privilege*. What then is our responsibility as we live it? It seems to me that we are to recognize the transitory nature of life. We are to open all of our senses so we can experience the wonder of the world. We are to build loving relationships with one another. We are to be grateful for the incredible gifts we have been given not tomorrow but today. For no one of us knows how many mornings we will have.

14

Janette Rainwater wrote a book over forty years ago that still has relevancy for our living today. In *You're in Charge,* Dr. Rainwater asserts that each of us can become our own therapist. There are two magic questions she proposes we ask ourselves.

First: "What is happening right now?" What am I thinking, feeling, doing? How am I breathing?

Second: "What do I want for myself in this new moment?"

We can't blame our living on someone else. Change, Dr. Rainwater instructs, happens when we accept who we are and become cognizant of the reality that *we* are in charge. What a gift it is to be able to change and to make those choices that will help us be more fulfilled as human beings.

What changes do you want to make for yourself?

15

On August 8, 2022, actress and singer Olivia Newton-John died at 73 years old. First diagnosed with cancer in 1992, she spent decades battling recurrences, yet she remained an optimist by choice. Her words about living stay with me: "I try to live in the moment and enjoy right now, which is all we have."

We can choose to become stuck in the past, living with regret, guilt, and disappointment or we can become paralyzed worrying about an unknown future. Let's give a gift to ourselves. Let's celebrate the now, living our moments with awareness and thanksgiving.

16

"I'm now 59 with Stage 4 metastatic breast cancer. I still don't have a partner, but I've fallen desperately in love with life. Exquisite beauty emerges everywhere: my cat on my lap, a cashier extending an unexpected smile, sunlight skipping across a lake."

Clare Cory

When I read Clare Cory's words in the May 26, 2024 issue of the *New York Times* article "Tiny Love Stories", I was touched. In the face of death, Cory finds beauty in life's small moments. Her story encourages us to take stock and recognize the magic that infuses our everyday. Her experience shared, becomes a gift, a reminder that no matter what we are going through, if we look, there are sources of joy, comfort, and wonder all around us.

What are the small but wonderful things that keep you going and make you fall in love with life?

17

"Every day we are engaged in a miracle which we don't even recognize: a blue sky, white clouds, green leaves, the black, curious eyes of a child—our own two eyes. All is miracle!"

Thich Nhat Hanh

In *The Miracle of Mindfulness*, Buddhist monk and peace activist, Thich Nhat Hahn, reminds us to recognize the miracle that is life. As it does for Thich Nhat Hanh, the wonder of this miracle often comes into focus for me in the natural world. It makes no difference whether I am looking out at a massive, sparkling iceberg in Alaska or stopping to watch a cardinal visit the bird feeder in my backyard. I am filled with awe and gratitude.

What do you count among the wonders of existence? When did you last give thanks for the miracles all around you?

18

I'm not ashamed to admit that I am a big fan of Hallmark movies. Some people find them sappy and overly sentimental, but I appreciate how unabashedly they celebrate love and kindness. They offer an optimistic view of the world that I can't get enough of.

In the Hallmark film *Journey Back to Christmas*, Toby asks Hanna: "What's the difference between a miracle and something that just . . .happens, like rain? Is rain a miracle?" Hanna responds: "Maybe everything is a miracle—rain, comets, you, me. It just depends on how you look at it."

Do you see the miracles in what is too often considered the ordinary? Open your senses in the present moment to recognize all that is extraordinary in the sacred experience of life.

19

While in active ministry, I visited a man dying from a complicated heart issue. He shared with me that he was not afraid to die. In fact, he viewed death as an adventure. I was struck by the idea of experiencing *all* of life as an adventure. What a dynamic way to live—to face each day with a sense of possibility, eager to see where the road will lead us.

This is a day for adventure. Walk your path with light, peace and love.

20

"Through many dangers, toils and snares, I have already come; 'tis grace hath brought me safe thus far, and grace will lead me home. The Lord has promised good to me, his word my hope secures; he will my shield and portion be as long as life endures."

Amazing Grace by John Newton

Faith defined as trust is a foundational gift. It sustains us during the crises of the journey. Trust in a loving God can give us hope and meaning when a loved one dies or when there is a financial setback, when an illness unexpectedly brings chaos into life, or a child is seriously injured. A firm faith sustains us and gives us strength and comfort.

In poetic fashion, the lyrics of "Amazing Grace" affirm: When we laugh, God laughs. When we cry, God cries. God is present with us always.

God is with you even now.

21

In 2023, Surgeon General Vivek Murthy released an advisory identifying loneliness and lack of social connection as a public health crisis in the U.S. Whether this crisis was precipitated by COVID-19, social media, a societal imperative to stay busy with work, the breakdown of the family structure, or, more likely, some combination of factors, the fact remains that many of us are suffering.

For those of us who are not currently experiencing loneliness and disconnection, chances are we have at some point in our lives known these feelings. Let us be the wounded healers who can, for a time at least, help dispel someone else's feelings of alienation.

Make a concerted effort to be present with another person and listen to their story, even if it's just for fifteen minutes. Offer acceptance and understanding.

22

I believe we are fulfilled as people when we assist someone who is hurting. We are all broken in one way or another. As wounded people, we have the experience and capability to be present to others who are struggling, to lend care and compassion to those in need.

I think of Vicki, a mother of two young children, who was dying from melanoma. Her friends and neighbors reached out to help. They provided meals, childcare, visits, and transportation to help alleviate some of the responsibilities of daily living.

Vicki's spirit was lifted by the generosity and care by her community, and those who contributed to the human care package given to her also felt blessed. In Vicki's final days, they had been able to provide her some peace and comfort, to let her know in no uncertain terms that she was loved.

Be a gift giver.

23

Watching the television show Chicago P.D. during a lunch break I took note of an exchange between two characters. Sgt. Voight says to Hailey, "You're in control so marvelously well."

Think about that comment for a moment. Are you in control of your life? Are you at peace with yourself? If not, what are you going to do about it?

Claim your life. Become that person you want to be.

24

*"The melody of each generation
emerges from all that's gone before.
Each one of us contributes in some
unique way to the composition of
life."*

Fred Rogers

Have you ever considered that your life makes a difference? All of us have gifts we can live that will make our communities and the world a better place. No act of kindness is too small. No act of caring is inconsequential.

25

The major religions of the world stress the ethical imperative to love. It is that which connects us to the absolute and enables us to realize our fullness as human beings. Love is not just a nice idea. Love is an action-oriented verb. Love involves praxis.

What holds you back from giving the gift of love? How can you put love into practice every day?

26

*"Be a rainbow in someone else's
cloud."*

Maya Angelou

What a gift it is to realize that all of us are capable of
bringing some warmth, sunshine, and love into
someone else's life. Be a rainbow today!

27

Every year on my birthday, I take a moment to stop and reflect on the occasion. The day never feels different than other days, but I recognize it as a milestone that deserves to be celebrated. I am quite aware that none of us know how many more birthdays we will have.

So, the question becomes: how will I celebrate my birth? With family and friends, cake and ice cream, certainly, but also, with gratitude for the miracle of my existence, the richness of my life, and the privilege of another day. I challenge myself to express that gratitude not only in words and thoughts, but also through my behavior and actions.

Celebrate the gift of your life by sharing your gifts with others.

28

We often try *not* to think about the end of our journey. But I find that pondering death can help us live with more meaning. Consider how you will be remembered when you are gone.

Why not take a few minutes and write your own obituary? When you have completed your reflection, ask yourself: Am I modelling the values I have described? Do my actions match my intentions? Am I sharing the gifts I want to pass on to others?

Live your legacy *now*.

29

My wife and I experienced a violent storm. The rain descended in torrents; trees were falling, and roads were flooded. As we watched the news accounts of the happenings, our electricity abruptly went off. We spent the rest of the night in darkness, relying on a flashlight to navigate through the house. The electric company indicated we would have no electricity until 11:00 p.m. the next day. Yuck!

How we take our comforts for granted. We take the stability of our living conditions for granted. We too often fail to recognize what we have until it is taken away. What if we were to give thanks on a daily basis for all that we have? How would your perspective shift if you lived every day with an attitude of gratitude?

30

" 'Tis the gift to be simple, 'tis the gift to be free, 'tis the gift to come down where I ought to be; and when we find ourselves in the place just right, 'Twill be in the valley of love and delight."

Simple Gifts by Shaker Elder Joseph Brackett

Joseph Brackett's lyrics date to the nineteenth century. Over 250 years later, the words continue to speak to me, especially as I grow older. When I stop and really see all the stuff I have accumulated over the years, I yearn for greater simplicity.

When we talk about gifts, we often think about something we get. But it can also be a gift to let go of something. To be less encumbered by material things is freeing.

The next time you want to treat yourself, try decluttering. Get rid of what you do not need. If you can give it to someone else who does need it, even better.

31

Leo Buscaglia, a writer I have turned to many times for wisdom over the years, asks this question: "Why do some people always see beautiful skies and grass and lovely flowers and incredible human beings, while others are hard-pressed to find anything or any place that is beautiful?"

Which kind of person are you? Which do you want to be?

32

*"I see trees of green, red roses too. I
see them bloom, for me and you. And
I think to myself, what a wonderful
world."*

*What a Wonderful World, written by
George David Weiss and Bob Thiele,
performed by Louis Armstrong*

I read a letter from a minister who quoted these lyrics
from Louis Armstrong's "What a Wonderful World." I
hadn't heard the song for some time, but as I read
them, I began to sing. Not out loud mind you but
inside. In the midst of everything that was going on
that day, the words reminded me to stop and
appreciate the wonder of life.

Take a moment to stop, celebrate, and give thanks.
Sing along with me: What a wonderful world…

33

I think Earth Day should be every day. What a privilege it is to receive nature's gifts on a continual basis, to be alive and able to experience the wonders of the world.

As I write this, I am reminded of two memorial services I recently officiated for individuals who connected with the beauty of the earth in special ways. One man enjoyed sitting on his back porch and watching the birds at the feeder. Another gentleman loved to walk along the beach and pick up shells. How about you? How do you connect with the earth?

34

I had a mountaintop experience on Wild Cat Mountain in New Hampshire. I joined family and friends for a special wedding. Waiting for the wedding to begin, I became lost in the beauty of nature. In that place there was majesty and miracle, quietness and calm, connection and love.

What a gift it is to see and experience the magnificence of the natural world. We have gifts around us all the time if we live with awareness and gratitude.

Have you had a mountaintop experience of your own?

35

My wife and I were fortunate to be able to travel to Costa Rica on vacation. While there we enjoyed seeing sloths in their natural habitats. Before we left, my wife bought a shirt with a picture of a sloth and the words "Slow down" on it. It was a great reminder to bring home with us.

So many of us live hectic lives with lots of responsibilities. We rarely take the time to appreciate the moment we are in. As we speed along, we often miss the colors around us and the potential to connect with others.

Give yourself a gift. Slow down, my friend.

36

*"Whatever you want to grow, tend to
it. Whatever you don't like, prune it.
You're the gardener of your life. Don't
let people tell you otherwise."*

Stefanos Xenakis

Reflecting on whether life has rules. In *The Simplest Gift,* Stefanos Xenakis concludes that it does and one of them is looking after yourself. He uses the metaphor of the garden to make his point.

We have control over the gardens we grow. How is it with your garden?

37

As humans, we have been given the gift of choice. We can give light in dark places, or we can choose to be part of the darkness. Think about it. We have the power to be better people. We are capable of formulating resolutions and making them real in the context of daily living. This kind of change can be difficult—it requires awareness, motivation, and hard work, but the payoff is immeasurable. The first step is choosing to commit to the change.

Using the gift of choice, make a plan to become the person you want to be. What changes would bring you greater fulfillment and contentment?

38

"We are our own worst enemies. No one does a better job of deceiving us or treating ourselves badly than we do. No one can do a better job of finding ways to ignore our innermost thoughts and fears than we can."

J. T. Garrett and Michael Tlanusta Garrett

This powerful statement stayed with me after I read the Garretts' book, *The Cherokee Full Circle*. We do ourselves so much harm through our inner dialogues. But we can decide to give ourselves a gift, a life-changing gift. We can replace negative thoughts with positive comments about our worth and dignity.

Pay attention to the messages you are sending yourself. When you catch yourself beating yourself up or tearing yourself down, make an active effort to offer yourself love, compassion, and forgiveness instead. You are special; you have cosmic value.

39

While getting off my bike last summer, I fell. I was lying on the ground with my bike on top of me when a man walking his dog rushed over. He asked if there was anything he could do. Stunned by the fall, I simply reached up with my hand. He took it and helped me to my feet. Then he picked up my bike and offered to assist with whatever else I might need. Fortunately, I was not seriously hurt.

It is a gift to be able to help others, but it is also a gift to recognize when we need help and allow ourselves to receive it when offered.

Who has offered you a helping hand? Did you take it?

40

"There's no such thing as an entirely 'weak' or 'strong' person. There are human beings, each perfectly imperfect, all sharing one path on this journey we call life. And along that route, we hurt. We cry. We grieve. We sometimes show our sore spots. That display, I've learned, is not an indignity. It's a superpower."

Robin Roberts

The gift that Roberts writes about in this passage from *Brighter by the Day* is often one of the hardest to give. But it can also be one of the most rewarding when we do. It is vulnerability.

Embrace your superpower!

41

I never thought about a mistake as a gift until I read Steve Leder's book, *For You When I'm Gone.* Leder quotes a friend: "I have always tried to take each mistake and cherish it. It's win-win: the more mistakes you make, the more gifts of learning you will have; the fewer mistakes you make..."

Making mistakes is part of the human experience. Think about a mistake you made. What did you learn from it?

42

There is a picture hanging on the wall in my home. A lovely red flower grows in the midst of weeds. A statement beside the blooming flower reads: "Perhaps strength doesn't reside in having never been broken but in the courage required to grow strong in the broken places."

No doubt all of us have been wounded or broken by our own actions and those of others. This is the reality of the human experience. But so is our ability to give ourselves the gift of healing and forgiveness, to learn from the past and allow ourselves to live more fully in the present.

43

A friend recommended I watch *The Resurrection of Gavin Stone* on Netflix. Gavin, the film's central character, has had a rough journey. Assigned to community service at a Baptist church, he finds himself cast as Jesus in a theatrical production.

In the play, Jesus, encounters a crowd debating the fate of a woman accused of adultery. The crowd, insisting that she has intentionally broken the law, believes she should be stoned to death. But when they ask Jesus what the appropriate sanction should be, he kneels down and writes with his finger in the dusty earth one word: Grace. It is a transformative moment for Gavin, who is himself searching for a second chance.

We all make mistakes, behave inappropriately at times, do things we know we should not do. We are, after all, human. As humans, don't we also deserve the gifts of acceptance, forgiveness, and love? How often do you give these awesome gifts to others? When is the last time you gave them to yourself?

44

I once came home to a dark house and didn't turn on the lights. Having lived there for years, I figured I knew where everything was and could negotiate my way through the darkness. I then painfully stubbed my toe on a door frame.

Light helps us overcome problems and circumvent dangers. It brings us clarity and hope. We can each be a light in the world, helping those who fumble in darkness, illuminating paths for those who are lost in shadow.

Be the light: Offer the gifts of compassion, understanding and acceptance to someone struggling with fear, loneliness, despair, and emptiness.

45

*"What kind of woman do I want to be?
One who willingly gives and receives
love. One who is compassionate.
Understanding. Positive. Forgiving. A
woman who makes responsible choices.
I want to live with a heart open to life."*

Oprah Winfrey

Have you ever seriously contemplated what gives your life meaning? What grounds you? What are your priorities and values? What is your passion? What kind of person are you? What do you want your legacy to be?

It is a gift to be able to choose our life's path. Embrace it. Be intentional about your journey.

46

"The most precious thing you can give someone is your time, Chika, because you can never get it back. When you don't think about getting it back, you've given it in love."

Mitch Albom

Time is, as Mitch Albom reminds us in the book *Finding Chika,* a precious gift. Although we do not know when the clock will stop for any of us, we all have a limited quantity. It seems to me that we would do well to think about how we spend it.

We live in a culture that takes pride in being busy and constantly doing. But I would argue that time well spent needn't be time spent being "productive". It's a matter of balance. Giving the gift of time is a way to show love and care, for others and for ourselves.

Are you showing up for others? Are you taking time to be present with yourself?

47

Arthur Ashe, in his book *Days of Grace*, writes a letter to his daughter, Camera. He has a terminal illness and wants to tell her all the things he may not get a chance to—all the lessons he has learned in his life, all of the hopes he has for her future. At one point, he reflects on art and poetry. "Don't let anyone tell you that either is frivolous or expendable, or inferior to making money," he comments, "Without either, and music, life would be dry and without feeling… This gift is from God, and you should revere it in others and in yourself, if you should have it."

Art, poetry, music—these are gifts to be cultivated, given, and received with wonder and gratitude. Appreciate them. Share them if you can.

48

When I was ten years old, my aunt gave a Christmas gift to my twin brother and me. It was a metal picnic basket full of cookies. I must admit I was disappointed with the gift. I would have preferred a toy train or perhaps a puzzle; I expressed my feelings to my mother. She was not very sympathetic. I still remember her words: "Make sure you send a thank you note. It's the thought that counts!" Looking back, it was an important lesson.

When people remember us with a gift, no matter whether we need it or like it, we ought to give thanks. There is magic in the phrase "thank you". It shows the giver that we appreciate their thoughtfulness and generosity, and it reminds us that the best gifts are not things at all.

49

Every year on Memorial Day, Americans pause to remember those who have given their lives so that we can be free. Those who have sacrificed so that we might have the privilege to express our opinions openly, pursue our faith as we choose, and live as our authentic selves. I suggest that we honor them not just on a holiday but every day. We can do this not only by recognizing what a gift our freedom is but also by acting to preserve our freedom and using it in service of others.

Let's live with compassion, work for justice, and vote for those who understand that we are all equal members of the human family.

50

*"Great gifts mean great
responsibilities; greater gifts,
greater responsibilities."*

Luke 12:48, The Message

A friend and I were lamenting all the darkness, brutality, and poverty in the world. As we considered the suffering experienced by so many of our brothers and sisters, we affirmed and gave thanks for how fortunate we are in our own lives.

Jesus tells us that our responsibilities are to be proportionate to our gifts. Those of us who live in relative economic stability, enjoy physical safety, and have access to greater opportunity are called on to share our abundance, offer refuge, and open doors for others. How are you responding to the call?

51

Theologian Carl Michalson writes that love is a chosen attitude of respect for every human being. If we are to be loving people, we must struggle to accept, respect, and care for all members of the human family. We are not to exclude certain people because they are not like us. We are not to think that we are better than certain people because of their color, religion, ethnicity, or sexual orientation. Every person is unique, a special act of cosmic creation, and we are all connected to one another.

Each of us is worthy. Each of us is deserving of love.

52

Many individuals have jettisoned the institutional church because of what they consider hypocrisy— a failure to practice the messages of acceptance and forgiveness articulated so often in prayers and on signs.

In my own experience, I think of a church where a gang of youth regularly hung out on the doorstep. The church had a newly refurbished gymnasium but refused to let the young people in to use it. The trustees didn't want the floor scratched. I remember a church member who complained about the church being involved in societal issues. She wanted it to be an oasis away from the problems of the world.

We need to reflect on congruence in terms of our personal living. Do our words and deeds match? Striving for a genuine connection between our speech and behavior can help us realize our fullest humanity as we endeavor to be the best people we can be.

Do you live a congruent life?

53

To be able to think is one of the greatest gifts we have. Unfortunately, there are too many people who do not use it. We need to be thinkers! We need to challenge our beliefs and make sure what we believe is true for us. We need to reflect on our priorities, so we have no regrets. We need to ponder how we live our journey if we are to be our best selves. And then, if we feel uncomfortable with our beliefs, priorities, or behavior, we can commit to making the changes necessary to live lives of authenticity and integrity.

Stop *doing* for a moment and take time to *think*.

54

I'd venture to say that all of us have experienced
loneliness and self-doubt at some point on our
journey. At times like these, it is helpful to recognize
that we hold the keys to our own cells, to affirm that
the creative power of the universe makes "no junk". I
share with you a poem that I wrote when going
through a tough time:

Alone in a dreary cell
The door shut but not locked
Fearful of opening the door
Not risking the uncertainty
Of freedom and choice

Sitting alone in the darkness of despair
Focusing on failures, mistakes made
Negative thoughts from deep within
Clouding the sunshine, clutching pain

There is a way out of that lonely place
A way of escaping the numbing embrace
Just open the door, open the door
Walk into sunshine and freeing air

Push aside the fear that inhibits
Take the chance of positive thinking
Listen to your heart and move ahead
Don't falter and do not dread

Open the door, open it wide
No one is stopping you from the inside
Open the door and walk confidently out
Of the self-inflicted darkness and doubt

Write yourself a poem or a note that you can turn to
when you find yourself stuck in a dark place.

55

"Man can live the most self-fulfilling, creative, and emotionally satisfying life by intelligently organizing and disciplining his thinking."

Albert Ellis

While professionally engaged with students at various universities over the years, I found so many who were bright, affable, and creative and yet had a poor image of self. They were feeding themselves negative thoughts about who they were and causing themselves great harm. I tried to help them dispel this toxic thinking and replace it with positive messages.

Sometimes therapy or psychological support is needed to help us deal with low self-esteem or overcome the challenges of self-deprecation. But we all have the power to change our thinking and live self-affirming lives.

We are what we tell ourselves we are. Who are you? Do you recognize how special you are?

56

The Buddha is said to have taught: "You, yourself, as much as anybody in the entire universe, deserves your love and affection."

Too often, we focus on our negative aspects. We fail to affirm the positive, to give ourselves the self-love we deserve.

Why not give yourself a beautiful gift today? Look into the mirror and see your reflection. Don't pay attention to wrinkles or blemishes. Affirm yourself by repeating five times, "I love myself." Say it like you mean it!

You are special. You are valuable. There is no one in the world exactly like you.

57

Sometimes at night I like to unwind in front of the television. On one particular night, a furniture ad caught my attention. The slogan: "La-Z-Boy. Long live the lazy." Well, that's not a very helpful suggestion for a life's purpose. But it does suggest a meaningful gift we can give ourselves—and no, I don't mean a lounge chair!

In a culture that extols productivity and accomplishment, we would do well to remember that it's okay to take time for ourselves to recharge. Self-care is essential to well-being and allowing yourself to take a break from the grind can fuel inner rest, health, and a different kind of fulfillment.

Go ahead and give yourself the time to just be!

58

What is your happy place? Maybe it is an external experience you appreciate, such as sitting on a bench viewing the ocean or taking a walk on a lovely path through the woods. It might be working in your garden taking care of your beautiful flowers. It might be sitting in your favorite chair listening to your favorite music.

Your happy place may be an internal experience, a memory, perhaps, that you return to frequently because it connects you to a person you love(d). Your happy place might be nothing but focusing on your life-giving breath.

Whatever your happy place is, accept it as a gift. Visit it often and be filled with comfort, harmony, and peace.

59

Robert Fulgham, author of *All I Really Need to Know I Learned in Kindergarten,* reflects on the lessons of his early years. Among them: "Share everything. Play fair. Don't hit people. . .Say you're sorry when you hurt someone."

One that resonates strongly for me is this: "Live a balanced life. Learn some and think some and draw and paint and sing and dance and play and work every day." Good advice for all of us, don't you think?

What do you need to do to live a more balanced and contented life? What will give you the motivation to make a change?

60

An article in *People* magazine featured Michael J. Fox. Fox has been open about his struggles with Parkinson's disease. He has also shown us what it means to be a positive force in the world. Fox is a tireless advocate whose foundation has raised more than a billion and a half dollars for Parkinson's research. He is also, according to Tracy Pollan, his wife of thirty-four years, "one of the kindest people I've ever met." Pollan says that Fox "almost always looks at the situation and the people involved and thinks about others before he thinks about himself."

How do you deal with struggles and setbacks? Are there gifts you can continue to give even in the face of challenges?

61

Jay Wright was the head coach of Villanova University's men's basketball for twenty-one years. During that time, the Wildcats took half a dozen Big East Conference championships and made multiple NCAA Tournament appearances.

The players on Wright's teams believed they were blessed to have him as their leader. But it wasn't just because of his winning record.

Kris Jenkins, who hit the last-second shot to beat North Carolina in the 2006 national championship game, revealed one of the coach's greatest gifts to his players in a *Daily Times* interview. "The motto of our program is attitude," he said, "How do you respond when things happen to you in your life, things you really can't control, and what your attitude is moving forward? That's something I use every day."

What about you? How do you respond when things happen to you in your life? Could a shift in your attitude make a difference? Give yourself that gift.

62

In his book, *Better with Age,* Alan D. Castel urges readers to adopt what he calls the "ABCs" of successful aging—attitude, balance, connection. I find his ideas instructive, and I would argue that the ABCs are essential ingredients for a meaningful existence no matter how old you are!

What is your attitude toward life? Are you actively striving to achieve balance in how you live? Do you nurture connections with others? Mastering the ABCs takes practice.

63

Not too long ago, I was in a serious car accident and totaled my vehicle. Thankfully, no one was seriously injured. In the midst of this unanticipated crisis, I was touched by the gift of human connection. I received the gift of caring from the two people in the other car in the accident, from the people who stopped to make sure we were all okay, from the state trooper who drove me home, and from my neighbor who sent me flowers.

In the midst of all the ugliness in our world, there are those who live every day with warmth, understanding, and generosity. They make the world a better place, touching the lives of others with genuine humanity and bringing hope during times of despair. Are you a member of this "care party"?

64

My sensitive and loving sister, Dorothy, died on Thanksgiving eve 2017. I continue to miss my many phone calls to her each week. She was my road companion. When on a long trip I would chat with her, via Bluetooth, about so many things. Dot was one of my best friends who always supported me and would do anything she could to be helpful.

Whenever I see a beautiful monarch butterfly, I think of my sister, whose favorite hymn, "Hymn of Promise", contains these lines: "In the bulb there is a flower; in the seed, an apple tree; in cocoons, a hidden promise: butterflies will soon be free! In the cold and snow of winter, there's a spring that waits to be, unrevealed until its season, something God alone can see." Dot will always be with me, fluttering in my spirit.

Stop for a few moments and express thanksgiving for people who have touched your life with their encouragement and love. They have been amazing gifts to you.

65

Relationships bring connection and meaning to life. My wife, Kerry, has given me the most cherished gift I have ever received as a human being. It is unconditional love. Like all of us, I have flaws and have made some serious mistakes in my journey. Often, I am what might be described as "high maintenance"! The wonder of it all is that my wife loves me with all my idiosyncrasies and contradictions.

What a gift it is to give and receive love which fills the heart and makes the spirit leap for joy. When my days on earth have ended, I know that I will conclude my journey with celebration. Why? Because I have known the love that has made me whole.

Have you known or given unconditional love in your life? What did it mean to you? What would it mean to you?

66

We are often reminded to give thanks for the people in our lives, those who love and support us through our journeys. We would do well to also express gratitude for the pets in our lives. Animals can reduce stress, improve mood, and, according to new research, help slow mental decline in older adults. As I know from personal experience, a pet can also become an integral member of one's family.

My wife and I have a warm, friendly, wonderful dog, named Hope. Hope loves to swim in the ocean, enjoys her treats, and likes to lean against us when being petted. Whenever I come home, Hope is there to greet me with a wagging tail. Whether she knows it or not, she makes a difference in my life.

Don't take the special pet in your life for granted. Be thankful and return the unconditional love it gives to you.

67

After reading an article about Dr. Joseph Dituri, a researcher who set a record for living underwater—100 days at Jules' Undersea Lodge—I couldn't help but think about living above water. What enables us to live our days with contentment and fulfillment?

As human beings, we have many special gifts. One is that we can choose how we will face this day. We cannot undo the past, but we can make today a better day than yesterday. The way we perceive events is our reality. How we think about things makes all the difference in the world.

How will you make your day?

68

"You can give your money. You can give your possessions. But the greatest gift you can give is yourself."

Patrick Lindsay, Make the Most of You

The happiest, most fulfilled people, in my experience, are those who give liberally of themselves. They know that connection is far more consequential than things, that the greatest gifts are not monetary or material but are realized in relationship with other human beings. They live with deliberate compassion, empathy, kindness, affirmation, and love.

Why not give the world the amazing gift of you!

69

On Thanksgiving, so many of us sit around a table with friends and family to enjoy a sumptuous meal. We give thanks for who we are and what we have. We recognize that we are blessed. But do we also consider that we are to give as we have received?

As we remind ourselves to give thanks on a daily basis, let us also remind ourselves to share not just our material wealth but also our human gifts.

Ask yourself, do you listen to those who are hurting? Are you present for those who are lonely? Do you extend a hand to those who have fallen? Do you offer forgiveness to those who are trying to get back on their feet?

70

*"Kindness is rewarded but if you are
cruel, you hurt yourself."*

Proverbs, 11:17

When we make derogatory comments about another
person or fail to recognize or respond to another
human being in need, we miss an opportunity to use
our gifts for good, and often, in retrospect, we feel bad
that we have contradicted our own values. When we
speak harmful words or walk by on the other side, we
hurt ourselves. Through kindness, in contrast, we
manifest the presence of God.

Be kind.

71

In their book, *Me to We,* brothers Craig and Marc Kielburger recount a conversation with Mother Teresa. They asked her how she maintained hope when surrounded by sickness and death. "In our lives," she told them, "We can do no great things only small things with great love."

Sometimes we think we have to achieve something great to make a difference. We forget that we can make a difference through the little acts of kindness we share each day—listening to a friend in need, shoveling a neighbor's snow, saying thank you to the mail carrier, giving the waiter at the restaurant a special tip.

What small thing can you do today that will make a big difference in the life of another?

72

After preaching a sermon about the power of hugs at a retirement community, a resident told me she had not had a hug since her husband died two years ago. With deep empathy, I asked her if she would like a hug. In a soft voice, she said, "I'd like that." I gave her the gift. She cried. My heart was touched.

Not everyone is a hugger. But for those who are open to giving and receiving hugs, they can be incredibly meaningful. A hug can give us positive feelings and affirm our worth as the special people we are. It can help ease deep loneliness and comfort us through heartbreak and sadness. In times of joy, grief, or suffering, a hug can be good medicine.

Have you given or received a hug lately? Consider offering one or asking for one. If you are not a hugger, what other form of personal connection do you find affirming or soothing?

73

*"When you can't find the sunshine,
be the sunshine."*

Unknown

We live in a complex, confusing, and often dark world. It is tempting to get depressed, to feel hopeless, to wonder when someone else will step up to fix all the wrongs and make everything right. In these times, we forget that *we* have the power to be the change. We have the power to bring light to the lives of others through our empathy, appreciation, warmth, and love.

Claim your power. Be the sunshine!

74

"Do not let the world change your smile. Let your smile change the world."

Unknown

A resident of a retirement community once told me that she was an angel. Whenever she got on an elevator and saw a cheerless face, she would smile. Often, she told me, the person would smile back. The resident understood her smile as a gift of warmth and recognition that could make a difference in the lives of others.

All of us can be gift-givers through a smile. Let's smile more.

75

*"I can live for two months on a good
compliment."*

Mark Twain

Have you ever considered what a gift a sincere
compliment can be to another person? It can brighten
a day and make a spirit soar. Think of a time you have
received a compliment that had an impact on you.
How did it make you feel?

Recognize that it doesn't take much effort to let
another person know how much they mean to you or
how much you appreciate something about them.
Give the gift of compliments freely.

76

86

Norman Cousins reminds us that laughter is "inner jogging". Not only is it good for our own wellbeing, but it is also healing for others. I had a friend who was an amazing joke teller. At a conference some years back, he had me laughing so much that my insides hurt. Can you remember a time when you laughed like that?

77

*"Kind words can be short and easy
to speak but their echoes are truly
endless."*

Mother Teresa

What power words have! We need to think before we speak because our words can have significant impact on others. Negative statements can break a heart. But kind and affirmative words can make a spirit soar.

Use your words to lift up others.

78

We are reminded by Aesop that kindness makes a difference: "No act of kindness, no matter how small, is ever wasted."

Do you believe that every act of kindness is a gift?

79

*"It is one of the most beautiful
compensations of life that no man
can sincerely try to help another
without helping himself."*

Ralph Waldo Emerson

Kindness involves the intentional giving of oneself to help others, without expectations of mutuality, credit, or compensation. But that doesn't mean kindness isn't good for the giver as well.

Research shows that kindness has the power to boost satisfaction and happiness and foster more trusting and understanding relationships. It can also have positive benefits for physical and mental well-being. Acts of kindness release "feel-good" hormones such as oxytocin and endorphins, leading to a "helper's high" that can alleviate feelings of isolation, depression, and anxiety. Practiced regularly, kindness can decrease blood pressure and the stress hormone cortisol, too.

How does it make you feel to give the gift of kindness?

80

John C. Morgan, who taught philosophy and ethics, wrote a piece in my local newspaper. He offered several guiding principles for living. Among them:

Love more, hate less.
Treat others as you wish to be treated.
Take time for self-care.

Do you give the gifts of love and care to yourself as well as to others? Could you give more?

81

Watching NBC's singing competition show, "The Voice", I was impressed with the talent and commitment of the vocalists. All were passionate about developing their gift, putting in long hours and making personal sacrifices to become the best performers they could be.

Not many of us have an exceptional talent that will bring us public recognition. However, we all have gifts to give to the world. Consider the human gifts of compassion, acceptance, listening and empathy.

Are you doing all you can to develop your gifts? Are you sharing them?

82

*"This little light of mine. I'm going
to let it shine. This little light of
mine. I'm going to let it shine, let it
shine, let it shine."*

This Little Light of Mine, written by Harry Dixon Loes

A children's song reminds us that each of us can be a light in the darkness. Our caring, listening, loving presence can help someone who is unhappy, lonely, or grieving. By sharing our gifts, we can make a difference with our lives.

Let your light shine.

83

*"O Divine Master, grant that I may not
so much seek to be consoled as to
console; to be understood as to
understand; to be loved, as to love; for
it is in giving that we receive, it is in
pardoning that we are pardoned, and it
is in dying that we are born to eternal
life."*

The Peace Prayer of Saint Francis

At their core these words, attributed to St. Francis, are a variation of the Golden Rule most of us grew up hearing. What a gift it is to treat others with the love, respect, and understanding we wish to receive ourselves.

84

*"Aware of the suffering caused by
exploitation, social injustice, stealing
and oppression, I am committed to
cultivating loving kindness and learning
ways to work for the well-being of
people, animals, plants, and minerals. I
will practice generosity by sharing my
time, energy and material resources
with those who are in need."*

Thich Nhat Hanh

Buddhist monk, Thich Nhat Hanh, outlines the
principles of mindfulness training in *For a Future to be
Possible*. His statement about generosity, in particular,
resonates with me. In moments of reflection, we know
that we are fulfilled as human beings by what we give
and not by what we get.

Do you donate to compassionate causes? Provide food
to those struggling economically? Write letters about
social justice issues to policymakers? Volunteer to
help those with mental health needs? How do you
practice generosity in your life?

85

Every December as Christmas season approaches, I find myself reflecting on the seeming imperative to purchase gifts for the special people in our lives.

I recognize that material gifts are a way of expressing our love and appreciation for others and I always buy my wife presents, even when she tells me that there is nothing she wants or needs! But I am also aware that the most valuable gift we can give does not come from a store. It cannot be put in a box or wrapped up with a bow. That gift is kindness.

Genuine concern, warmth, care, presence, and understanding are the most powerful ways to show love and appreciation. The best part? Kindness is not a gift confined to a particular season or a single day. Every day can be Christmas when we give the gift of kindness. Make today Christmas.

86

Commercialism and consumerism are in many ways the hallmarks of our culture. We are bombarded with the messages: Want more! Spend more! Get more! It is not surprising that in this environment we cultivate greed rather than generosity.

In the Bible, Jesus tells the story of the rich fool who has a bumper crop and contemplates what to do with it. He decides to build bigger barns to contain the unusually large yield. He dies that very night. (Luke, 12:16-21)

Rather than expressing gratitude, the man in the parable thought only of his own profit. Rather than considering those who helped him realize his wealth or thinking to share his good fortune, he planned only for his own future.

What kind of legacy did he leave the world? What kind of legacy will you leave?

87

In conversation with friends, we acknowledge that things are really "messed up" at home and in the world. We wonder what can be done to bring light in the midst of darkness? Our answer, more often than not, is a challenge to ourselves to live with integrity, to speak and act in support of our values, to share the gifts of compassion and understanding with our fellow humans. This might look like writing a letter to the editor of a local newspaper, meeting with one of our representatives, or attending a protest. It must include voting for those who will shape a brighter future.

Are your actions in the world in alignment with your values? Do you speak out for what you believe to be right and just? How do you find and give hope?

88

*"Returning hate for hate multiplies
hate, adding deeper darkness to a
night already devoid of stars.
Darkness cannot drive out darkness;
only light can do that. Hate cannot
drive out hate; only love can do
that."*

Martin Luther King, Jr.

The words of Reverend King stir us even now, more than fifty years after his assassination. They speak to us in a world that continues to struggle with hostility, injustice, and war. They are a gift from a man who quite literally practiced what he preached and gave his life in the service of making the world a better place.

Reflect on the gift. Be inspired and challenged to practice peace, respond with love, and give off light.

89

*"My deeds must be my life. When I
am dead, my actions must speak for
me."*

Stephen Girard

All of us teach by example. A friend of mine was a chronic smoker. She repeatedly told her children: "Don't smoke! It's a dirty habit. It's like kissing an ashtray." Guess what. All of her kids smoked. What we say means little if we do not act in accordance.

The way you live your life is a gift to others. How is it with you? Do your words match your deeds?

90

A well-known former college football coach, Lou Holtz used to give his players two pieces of advice that resonate with me: Be the best human beings you can be and do no harm.

Striving to do our best with our time, talents, and resources is an extraordinary gift we can give to the human family. Of course, we all make mistakes at times and, whether intentionally or through acts of omission, we cause harm. This is part of what it is to be human. It is how we learn from our missteps and make amends for the damage we do that matters.

Ask yourself: Are you doing all the good you can? Are you being the best person you can be? How can you do better?

91

*"Life is what you make of it and
what you make of it is up to you."*

Old Adage

I remember a time when I was in college, fretting about a history exam I was not prepared to take. I focused so much on failing that I fed my anxieties until I was physically ill.

Have you ever paused to ponder how you create your world through your thinking? A positive view liberates us to live with purpose, peace, and joy. A negative view fosters pessimism, negativity, and despair. Positive thinking often contributes to good health. Conversely, through negative thinking we can, as I did, make ourselves sick. What a transformational gift we give to ourselves and others when we approach life with a smile instead of a frown.

How do you want to live your life? What kind of thinking will it take to be the best version of you? To change the world for the better?

92

At Christmastime, I often find myself lost in the lights on my tree. They become a source of meditation. The fleeting thoughts that constantly bombard my mind are put aside. Nothing exists but the twinkling lights. I am centered and connected to the universal calm. I experience an internal peace.

What centers you?

93

*"We have finally mastered the meaning
of Christmas when Christmas becomes
a way of life."*

Leo Buscaglia

Leo Buscaglia tells the story of a Christmas that almost wasn't. Leo had gone to the hospital for a physical exam during his winter break from university. While there, he had a massive heart attack. An emergency quintuple bypass saved his life. His Christmas that year was spent recuperating in the cardiac ward.

The experience was a wake-up call. Leo reflects: "At some time, still unknown, I might not be as fortunate as I was in 1982. But it is useless to dwell on that. Rather, I will accept the challenge it suggests to make the rest of my life a Christmas celebration. I still have years ahead of me for giving, sharing, caring, accepting, and loving."

Leo's words challenge all of us to live every day in a holiday spirit.

94

As a minister and a professor, I have often considered the meaning of religion. One definition that I used in my course on World Religions is this: "A community of people living out their convictions about what matters most in life and expressing it in creed, code, and ceremony." Another definition, favored in Western cultures, deems religion as a "set of beliefs having to do with the gods, through which one is taught a moral system." But the definitions that strike me as the most profound are those that ground religion in action.

For example, Micah, the prophet, defines religion in this way: "Do what is fair and just to your neighbor, be compassionate and loyal in your love, and don't take yourself too seriously—take God seriously." The Dalai Lama says simply, "My religion is kindness."

How would you describe your religion in terms of human gifts?

95

"Perhaps love is like a resting place, a shelter from the storm. It exists to give you comfort. It is there to keep you warm. And in those times of trouble when you are most alone, the memory of love will bring you home."

John Denver

Love is one of the most amazing gifts you can give to another human. It is one of the most amazing gifts you can receive. Its power transcends the here and now. Even the memory of it, as John Denver's touching lyrics suggest, can be enough to make a difference in a life.

What is love to you?

96

"I am of the opinion that my life belongs to the whole community, and as long as I live it is my privilege to do for it whatever I can...Life is no 'brief candle' for me. It is a sort of splendid torch which I have got hold of for the moment, and I want to make it burn as brightly as possible before handing it on to future generations."

George Bernard Shaw

I stumbled upon this passage when composing remarks for a funeral service I was officiating for a university president. The words perfectly encapsulated his approach to life. This man lived with a "we" mentality. He found meaning in working for the greater good and considered the impact of his actions not just in the current moment but also for those who would come after.

What about you? Are you living with a "me" mentality or a "we" perspective? Do you live your life as a brief candle or a splendid torch?

97

A new year is a time for reflection, an occasion for us to ponder how we are living our journey. But every day that we are alive can be a new beginning. Let's not wait for a specific date on the calendar to ask ourselves: Are we being the person we truly want to be? Are we making the world a better place through the gifts we share?

Tomorrow is a new day. How will you live it?

98

"People say that what we're all seeking is a meaning for life...I think that what we're really seeking is an experience of being alive, so that our life experiences on the purely physical plane will have resonance within our inner most being and reality, so that we actually feel the rapture of being alive."

Joseph Campbell

Take a few minutes and ponder Campbell's words. What makes you feel truly alive? What do you experience in those moments? How can you tap into that feeling on a daily basis?

99

*"God spoke today in flowers and I,
who was waiting on words, almost
missed the conversation."*

Ingrid Goff-Maidoff

One winter, my wife and I brought our hibiscus into
the house to protect it from frigid temperatures. I was
astonished when sixteen beautiful flowers burst forth
in bloom. They were mesmerizing. The big yellow
blossoms with their red interiors reminded me that
the world is full of beautiful surprises. All we need to
do is keep our eyes open.

Be on the lookout for unexpected gifts.

100

"My wish for you is that you continue. Continue to be who you are, to astonish a mean world with your acts of kindness."

Maya Angelou

We don't have the power to make everything perfect and beautiful in our world. We can, however, choose to be kind in the face of meanness. We can approach our relationships with compassion rather than judgment. We can champion peace over war.

When the world is at its darkest, don't give up. Lean into love.

ACKNOWLEDGMENTS

This book would not have been possible without the support and encouragement of Hank Winchester, a friend who challenges me to keep on writing. We connected while serving as Edgmont Township Supervisors.

I owe special thanks to my daughter, Jennifer, who spent hours editing the book as a Father's Day gift to me. What a wonderful gift! Jenn is a wise and insightful woman.

I am grateful to my wife, Kerry, who has listened generously to my many thoughts while composing the content of the book and always had helpful comments, despite having her own work interrupted!